The

Chosen

Answering God's Call

on your Life

Scriptures taken from the Holy Bible, versions NLT, NKJV, and NET.

Cover Design by: Hazel Cohen Tucker

ISBN-13:9781500795757

For more copies, visit www.Amazon.com.

Dedication

I dedicate this book to my Lord and savior Jesus Christ who is the head of my life, to my three children Jessica, Darnell, and James, to my grandchildren, and to my mother Mary Holmes who has always been an inspiration in my life.

Contents

Preface

"For many are called, but few are chosen." Matthew 22:14

"God loves you and has chosen you to be his own special people, so be gentle, kind, humble, meek, and patient. Put up with each other, and forgive anyone who does you wrong, just as Christ has forgiven you. Love is more important than anything else is. It is what ties everything completely together." (Colossians 3:12–15 CEV)

Answering God's call into the ministry in 1997 changed my life forever. Not only did He call me to do a particular work in the ministry, but He also chose me for the task. At the time the Lord called me to do His work, I was only twenty-eight years old. It was prophesied to me that what God had chosen me to do would not be the typical work of an evangelist, although He had given me the title evangelist, meaning one who spreads the "Good News" I was not aware that I was chosen to spread the good news to other ministers, pastors, apostles, and other deities of leadership. As the

6

Lord spoke to me, He showed me various situations that many church leaders are in. The Lord began to send me to different churches. While visiting and sometimes joining these church', I did not understand my purpose. In some cases, I would be a guest speaker and in other cases; He would simply have me become a part of the church to observe as He taught me everything He wanted me to know.

I am a firm believer that God confirms everything in our lives to us. One day, a highly respected apostle came to me and prophesied the ministry that God has called me to do will be for other ministers. The first thing That came to my mind was how was I going to speak to other leaders who were in most cases twice my age and some who have multiple church's and thousands of members? What was I going to say to them that they did not already know? Moreover, why me? All of these questions would be answered over the years to come. In addition to the Lord using me to spread the good news to His children and leaders, He also revealed something profound to me. God spoke to me and told me to return to school and obtain the

7

highest degree obtainable in psychology and counseling. The first question I asked God was, "How was I going to use this degree and how would my calling as an Evangelist tie together with psychology?" These are just a few of the questions I will answer in this book. I pray that you will be blessed by what the Lord has inspired me to write to you and I pray that God will be glorified!

Chapter 1: The Call

Answering God's Call on My Life

I was what some would call a typical Christian woman. I went to church every Sunday, I taught my children the word of God, and tried to be the best person I could be to everyone. During the summer of 1997, while proceeding with my usual activities at New Life in Christ Baptist Church in Greenville, SC, something began to stir in my spirit. I had zeal to do more than I was doing for Christ. A passion had begun to develop in my heart to serve God like never before. I wanted to do more. I wanted to sing more. I wanted to praise more. I wanted to direct the youth choir. I wanted to be a part of every positive work that was taken place within the church.

Then, I began to have dreams and visions. I begin to have what some might say where unusual dreams. I begin to dream about teaching the word of God. My dreams became so vivid that I could see myself standing in front of the congregation and teaching. Not long after the dreams, I begin to have visions and daydreams. I felt as if I were in another place, a place where it was just Jesus and me. I was led by my Spirit to read the word more. As I begin to read and study the word every day, the Lord would give me scriptures to study. I was not sure as to why I was receiving what felt like an extra dosage of anointing, but every day the dreams and visions continued. I begin to feel as if not everything I was doing in the church was sufficient. My then husband was also an active member of the church. I begin to push him to do more. I remember practicing songs at home with him to sing during what was called at that time, "devotion" of the service, a time of singing and testimonies at the beginning of Sunday morning service. I remember talking to my then hus-band one day and telling him, "I think God is calling you to preach" I recall telling him to study his bible more, read more, pray more, and listen to the voice of God. I even begin to pray for him that God would use him in the ministry and pray that he would answer the call to preach. One of the first things Christians will do when the Lord is calling them to do a work, is push someone else in front of them, and try to escape the calling. One day while I was on my knees praying for my husband to preach the word, the Lord spoke to me. He spoke bold and very clear. He said, "I'm not calling him; I'm calling YOU!" The sound was like a parent who had become frustrated with their child. I did not know what to say, I did not know what to do. I got up off the floor, sat on the edge of my bed, and begin to talk with the Lord. The first thing that came out of my mouth was, "ME? Why ME?" Then, I begin to ask God for forgiveness for my disobedience to him. I did not want my father angry with me. After asking for forgiveness, I begin to ask God for direction. I asked the Lord what He wants me to do. What does He want me to say? Again, He led me to the scriptures. I can recall feeling confused. I wanted to be obedient to God, but at the same time, I did not know if I was the right person to be speaking in front of a congregation. After all, my life was not one that had been perfect. I had many trials, obstacles, and sins that I felt would disqualify me from ever preaching the gospel.

In spite of my past, I made up in my mind that I would discuss this with my senior pastor. I went to him and told him what the Lord was calling me to do. He listened as always. Then he said to me "Why don't you read scriptures during devotion" I thought to myself. Ok. I can do that. That following Sunday, while leading what was then referred to as devotion; I pulled out my bible and read scriptures. It was a little different from the usual singing, praying, and testimony. To me, this was a way I could read the word without stepping into the pulpit. I went home and that night, the Lord woke me up out of my sleep, and again His voice was very clear. He said, "That is not what I told you to do," and I started crying. I knew when the pastor told me to read scriptures during devotion that it was not what God told me to do. Again, I was trying to escape the calling on my life. I found myself seeking answers from other ministers. I remember asking one Apostle, what would happen to a person if they knew God is calling them to preach His gospel and they do not do it. He just looked at me and said, "You're heading for trouble." He explained to me that anytime God asks you to do something and you refuse to do it, you're heading for trouble. I felt as if I was searching for someone, anyone, that would say to me, "Ree, it's ok if you do not preach." I never found that person. I went back to my pastor and said pastor I know what you have asked me to do in reading scriptures on Sunday morning, but that's not what God has called me to do. My pastor looked at me and smiled. He said the reason I told you to do that is to see if God was truly calling you to preach because when God call you to preach then there is nothing that anyone can say or do to keep you from doing what God is calling you to do. My pastor told me to continue to pray and seek God for direction. Then, he said something that I was not so sure I wanted to hear. He said, "Let me know when the Lord instructs you to do your initial sermon." He prayed with me and I went home and continued to study.

I would read and study the word every day. I talked with God about my fears. I explained to God that I was young (as if He did not know) and was not sure that I could do the work that he was calling me to do. He then told me to read the book of Jeremiah. As I begin to read Jeremiah, I felt as if God was speaking directly to me. My late father was also a preacher, similar to that of Jeremiah's father. I had always felt as if I were different from my siblings. In many ways, I was. I did not like being different. I remember always wanting to be like my older sister. She is so outgoing. I remember wanting to be like my brother, he is tough and does not back down in a fight. I was nothing like them. I was soft-spoken, shy, and in most cases, would walk away from a fight.

In my youth, I was always somewhere hurdled in a corner reading the bible, singing, going to church with friends, and always tried to please everybody around me. I was teased a lot as a child for being so different, but as I talked with the Lord and told Him that I was not like most people, He said to me, "I chose you before I formed you in the womb; I set you apart before you were born." (Jeremiah 1:5, CSB). As I explained to the Lord that I was young and would not know what to say, He spoke to me and said, "Don't say you're too young." If I tell you to go and speak to someone, then go! And when I tell you what to say, don't leave out a word! I promise to be with you and keep you safe, so don't be afraid" (Jeremiah 1:7-8 CEV).

Evangelist Ree Holmes-Monserrate

I begin fasting as I searched answers from the Lord. I asked the Lord when He wanted me to speak. I did not receive an answer right away. Several days later, He spoke to me and gave me a date. August 24th 1997. I went to my pastor and gave him the date. He prayed with me again and announced to the congregation that I would be preaching my initial sermon on that date. I informed my family and all of my friends. I stayed in the word constantly. The Lord revealed every detail to me. He even told me what to wear. I was to be dressed in all white and wear a white robe. As I begin to study the word He would have me to preach, I can recall wanting to write down everything I read, but God did not allow me to do this. I found myself trying to argue with God saying, "If I don't write this down, I'm going to forget when I get up there." Then He spoke to me again and said you will not be speaking, I will. I can recall writing down scriptures that He would have me to read during the message.

The closer the date came, the more anxious and excited I became. I was working for the State Health Department at that time and the ladies would tease me when I went in for work. They would jokingly make statements such as, "Ree, you are just gonna float right off to heaven." My family was also excited as to what was taking place in my life. The week of August 24th, I fasted more than normal. I had to take time off from work to focus on the word and only the word. That Sunday morning I went to service as usual. I was scheduled to speak at five o'clock pm that afternoon. My mother prepared a huge meal of roast beef, rice and gravy, macaroni and cheese, collard greens, and corn bread. She wanted me to come have dinner before I spoke, however I had to inform her that I was fasting and would eat after service. At five o'clock the church was packed. All the associate ministers from our church were in attendance as well as ministers from other churches, my family, friends, co-workers, and even my supervisor from my job showed up. To this day, I cannot remember all the details of the service. When I stepped up to the microphone, led the church into prayer, and read the scriptures the Lord had me to read, the Holy Spirit completely took over! I was later told that it was a powerful message and many were blessed by the word and the message. I was then read the charge by one of the Evangelist in the church and I was then licensed as an Evangelist, by New Life in Christ Baptist church, to preach the gospel as God has called me. On August 24th 1997, I accepted the call. What has God called you to do? Are you answering the call on your life?

Chapter 2: Preach the Word!

After accepting the charge and the call on my life to preach the gospel, I begin to preach as the Lord led me to do so. I became a regular speaker at New Life in Christ Baptist church. Every fifth Sunday was set aside for the women to speak. The Lord also used me to speak at outdoors events, and services. I traveled occasionally speaking the word whenever the Lord would have me to do so. I can remember one message the Lord gave me to speak at a church in Lincolnton, NC. My pastor and the members of NLIC accompanied me. Even though I was asked by various churches' and pastors to come and be a guest speaker at their church, or a speaker for various other programs, I always went to the Lord in prayer before I would say yes. There were times when the Lord would not have me to speak at certain places. I did not understand. I was licensed, on fire for the Lord, and ready to preach! When I did not understand He told me "Trust in the Lord with all your heart, and do not rely on your own understanding" Proverbs 3:5 (CEV).

Evangelist Ree Holmes-Monserrate

One thing the Lord showed me was this is not my ministry, but His. It was not my will, but His will. The times that I went to the Lord concerning preaching at a church His answers were always clear to me. If He said yes, He would give me the scriptures and a message. If He said no, well I did not go. Regardless of the position you are in, you will never be greater than the Lord Jesus. We must always seek permission from Him in everything we do. My children cannot give anyone the recipe to my homemade sweet potato pie, unless they first get the recipe from me. There are some today who are attempting to take the ministry of Jesus and make it their own. They are taking God's word and adding their own ingredients. We must remember that we are of Him, but we are not Him. We cannot preach our words; we must preach His word. Ecclesiastes 3:14 states "I know that whatever God does, it shall be forever. Nothing can be added to it, and nothing can be taken away from it." (Eccl 3:14 NKJV). We are not called to the pulpit to preach our opinions of others. We are not called to the pulpit to preach about people in society that we do not like. We are not called to the pulpit to build churches by stepping on the heads of others. We are called to the pulpit to PREACH THE WORD! So many have become lost in their calling and boast to the point that when they speak, others cannot hear Jesus over them. They read the scripture, but fail to preach the word. This is why so many people are wandering lost. They are seeking to hear from the Lord, but all they see and hear is man. My fellow preachers, the Lord inspired me to write to you and say to you. Preach the word!

We must always remember that the power we have comes from God. We do not have the power to wash away the sins of others, but God gives us strength and teach us to forgive others for the wrongs they have done toward us. What we have is a connection with the father through Christ Jesus, who has given us the word so that those who come to the churches and ask for forgiveness for their sins, their sins can be forgiven through their faith and ONLY by the grace of God. "The scriptures say that no one who has faith will be disappointed, no matter if that person is a Jew or gentile. There is only one Lord, and He is generous to everyone who asks for His help. All who call out to the Lord will be saved" (Romans 10:11-13 CEV).

While visiting various church's, I heard pastors, apostles, and other leaders challenge God. How were they challenging God? They challenged Him by placing restrictions and time limits on when and how Jesus would heal the sick and work miracles. I heard pastors tell members that could not walk, that Jesus is going to heal them and make them walk on a certain day. No one has been called higher than Jesus. No one has been given the authority to tell Jesus when He will do this and when He will do that. Now, this is not to say that they are not connected to Jesus. This is simply a message that no matter how big your church is or how many members you may have; God has not and will not give you the power to control Jesus. This is not to say that pastors and other leaders, as well as Christians who pray and fast for healing will not see the miracles of God. They will see the miracles in God's time, not theirs. I am a witness that there is power in prayer and fasting. I have seen people who could not walk, regain the use of their legs. I have seen people that were sick with various diseases receive healing from their diseases. Jesus gives us power as He gave His disciples power to heal the sick and to cast out demons; however, we must be willing servants praying, and fasting while we patiently wait on Him to perform the miracle.

I can recall a time when the Lord spoke to me and told me to start fasting for healing. At the time I begin to fast, I was not sure whose healing I was fasting for. He just said to fast and pray. A few days past and He spoke to me again and told me there was someone in the church who was very sick and He wanted me (during alter call) to lay hands on them so that He could heal that person. I still was not clear as to whom I would be laying hands on. I continued to fast and pray. Finally the next Sunday during alter call, (after obtaining permission from the senior pastor to address the congregation) I spoke to the church and told them the Lord spoke to me and said there was someone in the church that was in need of healing and He wanted me to pray for them. I then stated that if there was anyone in the church, who has been suffering from an illness to come forth to the altar. To my surprise, half of the

church walked up to the altar. There was even an el-
derly associate minister of the church that came off the
pulpit and stood before me to pray for him. I was in
shock. The only thing I could do was be obedient to the
spirit of God and anoint each one of them with oil, lay
hands on them, and pray for them one by one. That
night as I prayed and talked with God, I asked the Lord
why He didn't tell me it was more than one person.
Why didn't He prepare me to pray for half of the
church? His answer to me was, "I did." I told you to fast
and I told you to pray. If you would have known that
half the church was going to come to the altar, would
you have done the work I told you to do? This is what
He meant when he wrote in the book of Matthew
chapter twenty-four, verse forty-four "be ye ready at
all times" (NKJV) we never know when Jesus is going to
show up and use us to do His work. After that Spiritual
movement from the Lord and the conversation I had
with Him that night, I am convinced that Jesus has a
sense of humor.

The following week after anointing those who
came forth and the laying on of hands, members were

standing up and giving testimonies of how God had healed them. One by one, they testified. One gentleman, who had been on dialysis, testified that when he went to the doctor on Monday, they told him they did not find anything abnormal with his blood, and he no longer needed dialysis. Yes. I am a witness to the power of God! Did I heal those people? Not even! Was I obedient to God and did everything that He instructed me to do, so that he could work through me? Absolutely! The word, faith, works, and patience worked together for the healing of God's people.

The Lord continued to preach the gospel through me from the pulpit for the next two years. In addition to preaching, He was using me to provide spiritual counseling to members of the church as well as teenagers and to teach bible study in several local communities. Every aspect of my life is being governed by the Holy Spirit. Being led by the spirit, I left the NLIC church family. I love the church. I love the pastors and members, who happen to be members of my family; however, I had to be obedient to the spirit, which led me to join another Baptist church. I continued to preach the word, however the Lord sent me to that church to teach me. My journey as a student had begun. I felt like a child leaving home for the first time seeing as how I had been at NLIC since the age of seventeen. The Lord showed me the different characteristics of pastors and ministers. Not to say that some are better than others. We are all individual people with unique characteristics. I was able to attend a mission trip with the church, along with my then husband and my three children to Drew, Mississippi. The first thing I said when I stepped off the bus in Mississippi was, "it's hot down here!" It was so hot it took my breath away. I was told that we would be marching up several streets until we reach the church that our pastor would be speaking at. The first thing I did was pray. I thought to myself, I can hardly breathe in this heat, how was I going to march? Luckily, we only had to walk a few blocks, stopping along the way to invite others to join the service that was to take place. Overall, it was a good trip and I was able to meet some wonderful people. Our pastor preached the word. Many were blessed.

The Chosen: Answering God's Call on your Life

At the time I joined the second Baptist church, I was still working full time for the health department and I started a janitorial company. My plan was to obtain enough contracts so that I could resign my employment with the state. That would have given me more time to study the word, preach, and travel as the Lord would have me to do. Well my business got off to a great start. I had several professional contracts and was able to cut back on my hours at the office. This created a problem. I was now managing the same caseload at work on half of the hours in the office, I was also spending a lot of time hiring and training new employees for my janitorial company, not to mention I was very busy being a wife and mother of three. Eventually the workload became overwhelming and my health was being affected by the additional demands and stress that I had placed on myself. I had placed more on myself then I was capable of handling. The Lord gives us the desires of our heart; however, those desires may be more than what we are capable of handling.

Chapter 3: Panic Attacks

in the Ministry

In 1999 after working for the state for two years and just recently opening up my own company, I began to have problems with my health. I begin to have uncontrollable high blood pressure and anxiety attacks. My doctor placed me on several medications to control my blood pressure and medication to help with my anxiety attacks. One of the first questions I had for my doctor was what are anxiety/panic attacks? (I ask many questions, as you can see.) The answers in which I was given were quite vague. I was told that anxiety attacks are the result of the body releasing too much adrenaline at any particular time, however according to the *Diagnostic and Statistical Manual for Mental Disorders 3rd edition (DSM-III)* panic attacks are manifested by discrete periods of apprehension or fear which are accompanied by several physiological symptoms such as: palpitations, chest pain or chest discomfort, choking or smothering sensations, dizziness, vertigo or unsteady feelings, feelings of unreality, tingling in the hands and feet, hot or cold flashes, sweating, feeling faint, and trembling or shaking. These are just a few known symptoms associated with panic attacks.

As I continued to take on additional stress from work and new contracts for my company, my conditioned worsened. I had developed what is called panic disorder with agoraphobia. This was a more serious condition. My panic attacks had become more frequent. I was not able to pinpoint a stimulus that elicited the attacks. The attacks affected my ability to work. I had become afraid of having attacks when I drove, when I went into public places, and even when I would leave my home. I attempted to cover up my condition. I would take my medication to work with me. I would keep some of the medication in my car and in my van. My excuse for becoming so sleepy and lethargic throughout the day, (due to the side effects from the medication) was I was tired. I would always tell everyone, I was very tired and just need to go home and relax. Well of course that did not last.

Evangelist Ree Holmes-Monserrate

I took a trip to Washington, DC (my hometown) with my family. We decided to drive. My sister and I were to take turns driving. On our way home from DC, it was my turn to drive. As I started driving, I had a terrible panic attack. I felt as if all the cars were closing in on me and I could not get off the highway. I swerved into a small space just off the highway almost causing a terrible accident. The space was so small there was no room for my sister and I to get out of the van and change seats. She had to crawl over the seat to change places with me so that she could sit in the driver's seat. Everyone in the van was screaming as trucks whizzed by, with estimated speeds ranging from 55 to 80 miles per hour, shaking the entire van as they passed. My sister had a very difficult time regaining access to the highway from the small area in which my van sat. I began to cry and explained to my family that those attacks were severe and no matter how I tried to control them, I could not do it. I knew on that day, the Lord was protecting us. The space in which I ran off the road was just big enough for my van to fit in it. My sister was very angry with me. She said I should have told the family what was going on before I attempted to drive and she would have driven the entire way. She was right in saying so. Sometimes as Christians, we do not want to admit that we are suffering from various issues. There is a certain amount of fear that comes into the minds of Christians, especially Christian leaders. We feel that if we were to expose a problem within us, then others may view us as weak or not practicing what we preach. This fear is not of God.

The attacks became even more severe. I would have them on a daily basis and they seemed to have lasted longer. I can recall one day as I attempted to go outside and check my mailbox, as soon as I closed the door behind me, I started shaking and feeling as if I could not make it back in the house. My heart was pounding. I could see the mailbox, but could not make it. I quickly ran back in the house, went to my bedroom, and closed the door. After that incident, I had a very difficult time leaving my bedroom, let alone my house. I was always afraid I would have another attack. As my children would play outside, I would sit and watch them from my bedroom window. At that time, my bed–

room seemed like the only safe place in the world. In all actuality, my bedroom had become a jail to me. As I sat in the room day after day, I began to feel as if this was going to be my future. I had a full bathroom located just off my bedroom, so I showered twice a day, I would do my hair, and occasionally put on make- up as if I were going out. I was unable to preach at this point in my life. I had become angry with myself for allowing an entity other than God to control me.

During the months I spent in my apartment, I would read the word of God; I would clean the apartment, decorate, and re-decorate. As long as I can remember, I have always had what is now known as Obsessive Compulsive Disorder (OCD). I never liked anything to be dirty or out of order. I would often clean areas of the apartment that were already clean. My marriage had begun to suffer, not so much because of the panic disorder and agoraphobia, but my husband became both physically and verbally abusive. I prayed about the abuse I was suffering, however Due to the nature and extent of the abuse; I chose to become a single mother. This was not an easy decision, especially with me being in the frame of mind and condition I was in. It was a difficult decision, but the peace that God gave me in doing so was confirmation that I made the right decision. Was my life better after the divorce? Financially life was difficult, but there was peace in my home. That peace was priceless. Sometimes we must step out on faith and know that God has our back.

After my separation from my then husband, my family began helping me with my children and helping me around the house. My mom played a major role in helping me with my children and encouraging me to continue to press my way through life, even though I was having severe panic attacks daily. So... what was the underlying problem of the panic attacks? To this day, there is only speculation concerning the source. I was told that the attacks are the result of fear. The fear I felt was the fear of having another panic attack. I did not feel threatened in any way. I was still able to care for my children and myself. I cooked healthy meals, read books to my children, and played games with them. We were very close.

The doctors continued to treat the attacks with several medications. At one time, I was placed on antidepressants to see if they would help control the attacks. At that time, I did not know that taking an antidepressant when it was not needed could cause more harm than good. I had terrible side effects from the all of the medications I was prescribed. Finally, a doctor placed me on a high dosage of Alprazolam, which is tranquilizer. The medication was successful in helping to control the attacks and I was able to venture outside to play with my children and visit with friends. As time went on, God reminded me of what was needed for me to be healed. I immediately began to fast and pray. The doctors were able to gradually reduce the dosage, and eventually took me off all other anxiety medications. You see, healing is in the word of God. We must remember that no matter how serious an illness or situation is, God will always give us directions and instructions to receive healing.

As time went on, I became more comfortable with riding in cars with family and friends. I would have anxiety attacks; however, they were not as severe as they had been. I had a very close friend invite me to dinner with her and her family. I wanted so much to join them, but was afraid my attacks would return, so I declined her invitation. Later that evening she showed up at my apartment and insists that I join them. I was reluctant, but she was patient with me and explained to me that if I began to feel anxiety or uncomfortable, she would bring me home. I agreed and for the first time in over a year, I had dinner in a restaurant. That was a major break-through for me. God sent me help.

I studied the word of God more to see what the word says concerning anxiety attacks. What I found is that the word of God tells us in the book of Romans 12:2 we cannot allow the things of this world to control what we as Christians, do, act, think, or say. The word warns us to "not be conformed to this world, but be transformed by the renewing of your mind, that you may prove what is the good and acceptable and perfect will of God" (NKJV). By reading this word, as Christians, we must not allow things of this world to control our minds and that includes anxiety attacks, depression, and any other mental disorders. By changing the way I think about anxiety attacks, I am able to overcome them. This is the good, acceptable, and perfect will of God. Therefore, as we are instructed by God's word, anxiety and panic attacks may occur, however we can overcome them. Yes, there are days I still have anxiety and there are days when I feel panic, but the God I serve provides me with the strength to overcome them. Anxiety and panic attacks are real. They are associated with various unconscious fears, so where do they fit in God's ministry? They are used to teach the children of God that no matter what we face in this world; God is stronger and able to heal, if we give it to Him.

Chapter 4: Where is your Faith?

One of the most difficult concepts for many Christians to embrace is *faith*. Faith is, believing that God will work in your life when you cannot see the work he is doing. The word of God tells us that "faith is the substance of things hoped for, the evidence of things not seen" (Hebrew 11:1, NKJV). In order for faith to work in our lives, we must practice faith in everything that we do. It is easy for someone to say they know God will supply all of their needs when their needs are being met. It is the times when you do not have enough food to eat, or enough money to pay your bills, or your health is compromised that we must continue to practice and strengthen our faith. Christians have joy in our hearts and praise in our spirits when all is well in our lives. We must remember that on our most difficult days, we have to hold onto that joy and continue to praise the Lord. Praising the Lord through the difficult times will not only strengthen your faith, but will please Him. Hebrews 11:6 states, "But without faith it is impossible to please Him, for He who comes to God must believe that He is, and that He is a rewarder of those who diligently seek him" (NKJV). I do not personally know any Christian's who do not wish to please the Lord. Therefore, we should all be Christ-pleasing, faith practicing Christians.

There were times when I faced various illnesses that I did not understand why I faced these things, but I continue to trust God and have faith in His word that He will bring me out. I use the present progressive *He will bring me out* to say that I still face various illnesses. I have been diagnosed with rheumatoid and osteoarthritis and fibromyalgia. I cannot remember the last time I have had a pain-free day. Some days are more painful than others. There are days that I wake up and it takes me over an hour to stand up straight. My pain is severe, but my faith in God is stronger. I believe that no matter what we face, God is still in control and he will bring us out of pain and suffering in His time. The times when our bodies are afflicted with various pains, we should all think of Job. Known for his incredible patience and suffering, Job overcame his afflictions by clinging to his love for God and the promise that God would bring him out.

The Chosen: Answering God's Call on your Life

Years ago, when people would suffer from an illness, they were more than likely to take some form of home remedy as opposed to seeking medical treatment, and in more serious cases a trip to the local drug store would be in order. Modern medicine have coined terms for practically every form of sickness known to man. With the innovation of new diagnoses, come various forms of new medications. While it is true that a medical doctor can write you a prescription for any ailment, the word of God gives us specific instructions on how to deal with sickness and disease. James 5: 14-16 (KJV) tells us that if any are sick to call for the elders of the church to come and anoint them with oil and pray for them, the prayer of FAITH, that they may be healed.

How many of us are calling the appointed and anointed elders of the church to do the work they are designated to do? Do the elders of the church know the duties to which they have been commissioned to perform? Does the congregation know who the elders of the church are? In some church's, the elders are not called by God, but appointed by man. I pray that leaders of today are praying before appointing! Some may want the title, but not the responsibility. Every church in the world should have the answer to these questions. I have seen firsthand the results of those who become ill and do not know who the elders of the church are so, therefore they do not call and receive prayer and ultimately their healing.

Let's talk about healing for a moment. While I have witnessed people suffering from various illnesses and not calling to the elders of the church to pray for them, does not mean they do not receive their healing. The word of God and faith heals! When you apply your faith to God's word and allow the word of God to do the work, you can be healed. I am not an advocate for medications, but I know under certain circumstances, medications are necessary, helpful, and can be lifesaving, but even medication is useless without faith that God will use it to heal you. Where is your faith in times of sickness?

Faith comes by hearing the word of God, Romans 10:17 (NKJV). Are we as ministers, teaching, and preaching the word? It is easy for us to say to someone who is suffering hold on; your help is on the way, because those who study the word of God know that God's word tells us that He will supply all of our needs. As ministers of the Gospel, we have an obligation to teach what the word of God tells us about faith. I have heard it said that once we become saved, we are all teachers of the word. This is not so. Once we are saved, we should all become examples of the word. Becoming an example of the word includes; practicing faith, not only for yourself, but also for others around you who may lack faith.

Every Christian, especially ministers and pastors, should be exercising their faith both privately and publicly. I have sat in church services, heard pastors get up on the pulpit, and tell their listening congregation that they do not have enough money to pay the bills for the church building. I have seen pastors break down crying in presence of their congregation because they lack the financial means to care for the church and their families. I say to those pastors, "Where is your faith? If your congregation is witnessing you, the leader of the church, breaking down and begging for money, what are you teaching them about faith?" The answer to that is nothing! What you are teaching them is how to be successful beggars.

A successful beggar is someone who cries out begging others for financial or other help. They will use any scare tactics they deemed necessary to get people to give them money. The sad result is it works! The word of God tells us in Psalms 37:25 (NKJV) that "I have never seen the righteous forsaken," nor, His seed begging bread. How about Philippians 4:19 (NKJV) that the Lord shall supply all of our needs, and in Hebrews 10:38, (KJV) the Just shall live by FAITH! There is no need to cry, fall out in the floor, and threaten to close the church when church finances are low; all you have to do is apply your faith! I am a witness that God will supply all of your needs!

Faith should be applied to your daily walk with Christ, your relationship with your spouse and loved ones, and all areas of your life that require you to trust in the Lord. You may be seeking peace, understanding, your daily needs, both physical and spiritual. Apply your faith! Faith becomes difficult, when believers become inpatient. Not only do you have to believe God will do it, you have to be patient and wait on Him to do whatever needs to be done. Stop trying to dictate to God the severity of your problems. He already knows what you need and when you need it.

You may be going through a test. What if your electricity is turned off? Will you still trust and believe in God, will you light a candle and read your bible by candlelight? What if your car is repossessed? Will you continue to praise God while you are walking to work, school, or the grocery store? What if your body is stricken with arthritis? Will you praise and worship God through your pain? When you can't get out of bed, will you lift your hands and tell the Lord thank you for waking you up another day? These are examples of exercising your faith. How can I write these things? Because I have lived them! I have read my bible by candlelight, I have walked to grocery store, and I have praised God through my arthritis stricken body. There were days when my pain was so severe that I could not walk up the steps, but I praised God while I crawled. I am a witness that God has brought me through these trials every time. All I had to do was trust in His word and apply my faith! The question to leave with you is where is your faith?

Chapter 5: The Move

In the year of 2001, I moved from Greenville, SC to Spartanburg, SC. I did not understand why I chose to move 30 miles from my family. At the time of my move, I was extremely ill and my family was helping me with my children, who at the time were seven, thirteen, and sixteen years old. It was not until after I moved and had to depend solely on the Lord, that I learned how to depend on Him. Depending on God does not mean you pray about something, have faith that God will provide, and you sit down and do nothing. Depending on God means, you pray, apply your faith, and work! At that time, I was still having panic attacks, and little did I know, I was about to have surgery to remove my gallbladder.

I knew at the time I moved, that I wanted to become self-sufficient. I wanted to be able to care for my children on my own. I wanted to enjoy life again with my children. It was difficult being a single mother, but I do not regret one day of the time I spent with my three children. I refused to waste time, telling my children what they could not have because I was a single mother; I chose to show them what we did have. We had each other. We played board games, we played tennis, and we went swimming, and had backyard barbecues. I sat down with my children and night. I read books to them and did homework with them, I went on field trips, and never missed a recital or school concert. I was an active and loving mom, but had to also be the disciplinarian. Just because dad was not in the house, does not mean that a woman cannot raise respectful children. Remember Philippians 4:13 (NKJV). It was not easy, but it was not impossible. I give God all the praise and the Glory!

My move was not just a physical move; it was also a spiritual move. God moved me out of my comfort zone. I was visiting other churches and experiencing things that I had not experienced. I was meeting new Christians and various denominations of believers. It was not clear to me at the time, why I was being exposed to the things that I was, but if I had not the experience, I would not be able to write about it. Amen! It was during this time, after my move that I, a called, anointed, and appointed Evangelist, stepped out of the will and word of God and began to live an unhealthy lifestyle. I knew the activity that I was participating in, was not what God intended for my life. I was reminded daily by the Holy Spirit of my Sins. Again, I became angry with myself. I was ashamed to even talk with my friends. For a brief period, I shamefully walked away from the church, but God and the church that was in me, never left me.

I continued to read my bible and would cry after reading it. I prayed for forgiveness and answers as to why I walked away from something I hold so deep, which is my relationship with Christ. My panic attacks were now under control and I was able to return to work. I began to purchase cars, sport utility vehicles, and other material things. To someone who did not know me, would think I had, what younger people would say, "had it going on" A single mother, who is working full time, taking care of her children and her home, and getting all the things she needs, little did they know, I was miserable! I was not doing what I was called and chosen to do.

Finally, I asked God, "Why won't you take this sin away from me?" He answered me with a question. His question, in the small, still voice was, "Why won't you give it up?" God has the power to remove anything from our lives that is not of Him. It is up to us to give those things up and not look back on them. It does not matter what the Sin is. If what you are participating in is against God's word it is wrong. Sin is Sin. There are no big Sins and little Sins. They are all wrong! So, what did I do? I gave it up.

One of the hardest things to do is to give up something that makes you feel good. God could have taken certain desires from me, but He chose to give me the desires of my heart. Sometimes the desires of our hearts can lead us on a path of destruction. After repenting from my Sin and apologizing to God, my family, and to my children, I returned to my first love, which is Christ Jesus. I did not immediately return to the pulpit. I returned by humbling myself before God in the congregation. I knew that He would place me back on the pulpit in His time, not mine. God taught me a valuable lesson. We can have all the material things of this world, money, cars, and the best clothes, but without Him, we have a whole lot of nothing! The scripture Mark 8:36 (NKJV) remind us that it will profit us nothing, if we shall gain the world and lose our soul. There is nothing more valuable than your soul.

Now that God had forgiven me, I sat humbly in the church congregation and listened to His voice through other Apostle's, Pastor's, Ministers, Teachers, and Evangelist. Some of their teaching I could spiritually eat, and other's I could not because it did not agree with my spirit. There was a burning, so deep down inside of me to preach the word again. I wanted to get out and evangelize and do outreach, but I was careful not to move until God said so. In other words, I was placed on spiritual restrictions. My heavenly father was teaching me a lifelong lesson. This was not a restriction that I could come out when I thought I was ready to come out. This was not a five or ten min/day restriction. I was sat down for three years! I would attend Sunday school and would go home upset, because I believed that I would have done a more accurate job teaching the lesson. I never questioned God as to why I had to sit down so long, I simply thanked Him for forgiving me of my sins, and how He would use me in the His ministry.

As I was being taught, I was learning how to be obedient. Some ministers feel as if once they are in a position, they can do whatever they want. This is not the case. Remember we are not ministers of our gospel; we are ministers of God's Gospel. Pastors do not pastor their church. They pastor God's churches. Evangelist do not share our good news, we share the good news of Jesus. When you move into a position to minister the word of God, you are volunteering to give up your life, for a life of service to Jesus Christ. Ministry is not a job where you look forward to your paycheck at the end of the week. Ministry is volunteering your gifts for the glory of God. It is not written in the word of God that pastor's, and ministers are to receive a paycheck. When Jesus sent His disciples out to teach, preach, and heal the sick, He never instructed them to require payments in advance for their services. That is of man. Even as I write this book, I am not expecting to become wealthy from the work the Holy Spirit is doing through me. I am already wealthy. I have spiritual wealth that is priceless. If it is God's will that I am blessed financially, then I thank and praise Him for it, but even if I'm not, these are the words that He told me to write; to God be the glory.

The sad truth is some ministers and pastors will not give you the word of God free. They require a financial offering every time they speak. I have been among pastor's who have become angry that members have not paid their tithes or given offerings. It is not the pastor's duty to monitor who pays a tithe or give offerings to the Lord and who doesn't. It is not written that members are to write their names on envelopes as a way to monitor who is paying tithes and giving offerings. That is also of man. When you give unto God, it is between you and God. The word of God tells us in the book of 2 Corinthians 9: 6, 7 that we are to give from the heart, not out of compulsion and that God loves a cheerful giver (NKJV). If we love the Lord, we should freely give out of that love.

If members are free to give as they have to give, the churches would be full today. I have been in the presence of pastors who have had their members sign agreements on how much they will pay every week. If that amount is not paid, the pastor would become up-set. Some pastor's would even make phone calls as to why the members did not pay what they agreed to pay. Those pastors did not have compassion or empathy for those who lost their jobs and for those who were not able to pay. This grieved my heart and my spirit. I watched as families with small children would some-times run out of food, struggle to meet their agree-ments. These same pastors did not call the members to check on them, nor did they visit the hospital, or visit the sick. The only calls made, were to find out where the money was for that week. This was not Jesus' plan when he sent his disciples to preach the word. Jesus ministered to all. When we are called by God to minis-ter, this is not what He is calling us to do.

Some churches today have moved from God's plan to their plan. They have their own agenda. I have witnessed pastors who live with only the finer things in life at the expense of a few members with limited means. Pastors are dinning on expensive meals, and enjoy going out to eat with their families several times a week, while the members of their churches are starving and waiting in line at a local soup kitchen for a hot meal. I have witnessed families losing the use of their electricity to pay offerings in the church, yet the church leaders did not offer to help those families. Families who faithfully attend church services and will give their last to the body of Christ, families who are being taught by pastors that if you do not give a monetary offering you will not be blessed. Jesus blessed those who helped Him as well as those who did not. Giving time to the Lord and serving His people is just as important as giving money. Money will not last forever, but your labor and service of love will forever remain in the hearts of those whom you serve.

There was a time over 20 years ago when I sang on a choir. Sometimes I would sing lead and other times I would sing backup. We would go from church to church on Sunday and sing at various gospel concerts. There were no offerings taken up, just choirs from all around joining to sing praises unto the Lord. Today I ask, what happened to those times? Today they still have gospel singings and concerts, but now the tickets are so expensive many Christians cannot afford to attend. This is not to say that every church charge a fee for Christians to attend gospel concerts. This is an example of how many have left their first love, which is doing what is pleasing to God, to doing what is pleasing to them. Singing in the choir and with several other groups 20 years ago was to uplift and worship the Lord. Many groups today are simply giving other Christians a show. Many have been sold out to the almighty dollar and not to the Lord almighty. One of the most frequent reasons people give for not attending church services is they do not have any money. Sure Pastor's and leaders will tell them to come on anyway, but at the same time place guilt in them for not giving. This is not of God.

The message to the church leaders is this; churches cannot be built on the backs of the poor. If God desires for you to have a church building, He will provide a way for you, the pastor, to maintain it. He will also *send* you the help you need. Reiterating what was stated in the previous chapter, you cannot preach to the congregation, to cast all of their cares on the Lord, if you are worried as to how you will make the payments on the church building. When you see that you have more bills than income, which is the majority of Christians, not just pastors. Apply your faith and know that God will provide. Applying your faith does not mean preaching every sermon about giving more money. If God place in your heart to preach about giving every Sunday, then do what thus says the Lord! We are to make sure that we preach from Spirit and truth and not preach based on our personal circumstances. It is time to move from the mindset of what finances one has to give to the church and move into how the church can help you to overcome the sin in your life. What move is God telling you to make?

Chapter 6: The Non-Denominational Explosion!

After relocating to Spartanburg, SC I was introduced to the Non-Denominational church. My first encounter happened when I witnessed a non-denominational ministry as they had an outreach service in a community. The members were full of what appeared to be love for everyone. They provided a free meal for everyone in the community; they performed songs and dances for on-lookers. I was drawn to this type of evangelism. I have a love for people that can only be a gift from God. I desire to feed the hungry and provide clothes for those who are in need. I have a passion to serve God's people.

Being drawn to the non- denomination church, I was introduced to a lot of "first." While attending a non-denominational church, I saw members wearing blue jeans and miniskirts. This was a first for me. I was reared to always dress modestly when entering the house of God. I saw members wearing flip-flops and open toe sandals. Again, this was a first for me. I saw pastors displaying tattoos on their bodies, and multiple body piercings while preaching the Gospel. What I found most shocking was there were smoking sections in the back parking lots of some of the churches. I saw members, ministry leaders, and choir members smoking after service. The first thing that came to my mind was things have really changed or things are very different in the non-denominational church! I know that we all have our crosses to bear, but if you are going to lead, you must lead by example. If you are going to sing about the power of God, you must accept that power and allow the power that you are singing and preaching about to deliver you from sin and an unhealthy lifestyle. Our bodies are the temple of God and we must treat them as such.

As I began to research the non-denominational church, I discovered that we are simply a group of individuals who do not claim any particular denomination such as that of Baptist, Methodist, Pentecostal, or Apostolic to name a few. They do not abide by the same religious standards or services as other *organized* religious denominations. Growing up and even entering the ministry at a Baptist church, I was accustomed to certain parts of service. I looked forward to communion. Communion is a time for me as a Christian to remember what Jesus did for me. It is a time for me to reflect on the blood He shed for me and the bruises His body suffered so that I may live. I joined a non-denominational church without realizing communion was not something that all of the churches partake in. I knew I could not stay there.

Let's take a look at the word organized that I italicized in the previous paragraph. I used that particular word to say that from my experience in some non-denominational churches there was no order. The pastors of these churches do not practice the five-fold ministry as ordained by God. I have been in services where the pastor was, at times the praise and worship leader, he took up offering, did all the prayers, preached the sermon, and announced church activities to the congregation. This reminded me of Moses, who was warned by the high priest of Midian, "Jethro," who warned Moses that He should appoint elders to assist him. Moses was warned that he would become warn

57

out by taking on the sole responsibility to teach and ad-
vise the Hebrew people.

As a minister of the Gospel, watching the pastor
take on all the responsibilities in the church spiritually
wore me out! I did not understand why the pastor
would attempt to run the church by himself, when God
sent him ministers, teachers, evangelist, other pastors,
and apostles. This is the five-fold ministry that Jesus
gifted to man. Another pastor of a non-denominational
church refused to acknowledge the help that God had
sent him. He knew of my calling. He witnessed the
work that God has placed in me to do and even after
three years of attending his church, more than half of
the members did not know I am evangelist. They simply
thought I was another member who loved to praise
God and serve others. I was asked to do everything in
the church, except what I was called by God to do.
These are the types of limitations that many pastors
place on God's *chosen*. I have experienced pastor's asking my opinion of situations, then turn around, and
wrongly accuse me of wanting to take over as pastor of
their church. I have experienced jealousy from pastor's

and other leaders. When God showed me how man could become jealous of someone else's anointing, I was hurt. I will discuss this in a later chapter.

As I visited other non-denominational churches, I experienced much of the same. Many of the churches enjoyed participating in outreach programs, but denied the help that God sent them. One pastor even exclaimed that he does not like other ministers to preach from his pulpit. Again, here is an example of man attempting to control God. If God sent ministers to the church to assist you, you must trust that God will be in control. That type of flawed thinking, by pastors can cause you to lose the help that God sent you and cause you to become overwhelmed and burnt- out over issues that God did not intend for you to have. The reason Jesus gave the gifts to the ministry so that there would be order in the church. Those who reject the help that is sent to them by Jesus, rejects order.

I noticed that when there is no order in the church, members must have something to capture and keep their attention. From my experiences, non-denominational churches capture the attention of the members by providing a "feel-good" type service. These services have radical praise and worship, dances from various groups, and a brief message from the pastor. The services I attended were very much like this and lasted less than two hours. I have always been in churches where the Holy Spirit was welcome and free. There are pastors that time the services. Sometimes services for different reasons. Due to modernization, some services are broadcast online or via TV, therefore it is imperative that services be timed accordingly. If services are timed, then man is placing a limit on God. The Holy Spirit is not completely free if constricted by man's time limit.

Another first for me as I fellowshipped in the non-denominational church was to hear a pastor say that he does not want anything to do with casting out demons. I was confused about his statement and until this day, do not understand how a pastor, who is called by God to lead other's to Jesus, refuses to cast out demons. Refusing to cast out demons means you will allow demonic forces into your church. Be careful! These

60

demonic forces are not only after the one whom they possess, they are after the head. Not all ministers will cast out demons. Some even fear the process of casting out demons, but pastors are the head of the church. If the pastor does not believe in casting out demons and refuse to allow other ministers to practice their gifts in his appointed sanctuary, then many people will not receive what they go to church to receive, deliverance and healing.

Christianity has not changed. Respect for God and His sanctuary have. There was a time when I witnessed people being delivered and set free. Not to say that I am not seeing this today. I am seeing but through different context. There was a time when church services were moved toward the healing of the nations. Today we hear more sermons concerning becoming financially free than being spiritual healed. Sure, we would all like to be financially wealthy, but Matthew 16:26 reminds us that what does it profit a man if he should gain the world and lose his soul! (NKJV) Do not lose your soul trying to be become wealthy. Your salvation, healing, and spiritual peace are priceless. Your financial wealth cannot buy you a ticket into the king-dom. Just because you have taken denomination out of the church, do not remove the healing and power of God. You can be healed in blue jeans.

I must admit that not all of my experiences with non-denominational churches have been the same. I have attended services where the pastors did accept the five-fold ministry into the church. One of the things that warmed my heart was one particular pastor never emphasized paying tithes and offerings. In many churches pastors, place emphasis on giving at every service. Yes, they took up tithes and offering, however the pastor stated that whatever was in your heart to give, give and the Lord will make it enough. He did not require members to put their names on envelopes. He simply announced it was time to give unto the Lord. I saw so many people running with joy to give. They were excited as they placed their tithes and offering in the baskets. I also saw that same small church build a larger church with an outstanding outreach program. This truly touched my heart. Sadly, this was a single incident in my entire thirteen years visiting and joining the non-denominational church community.

I want to emphasize that not all non-denominational churches are the same. Just as every Baptist church is not the same, nor every Methodist church. They all have differences. My experience is many non-denominational churches relax their dress code. Many of the members attend services dressed casually comfortable. There is nothing wrong with dressing comfortable, however when we enter the house of God, we should dress in a way that is respectful to God and to His house.

When I began my walk with Jesus as a non-denominational Christian, I can say that there was an explosion within me! I was taken aback by many of their spiritual practices and beliefs, but it never changed who I am as a Christian and woman of God. I am still a non-denominational Christian who loves the Lord. My personal beliefs are this; the word of God will always be true. We are living under the disposition of God's Grace under the new covenant of Jesus Christ. I do not pretend to love others. I simply love them. I continue to partake in communion and minister the Gospel as I am led by God to do so. My walk with Christ is not about denomination, it is about Jesus, the love He has for me, and the love I have for Him.

Chapter 7: Stop, look, and listen!

There are times in our lives when things seem to be going in every direction except for the direction that we want them to go, or the direction we think they should be going. Ministers and pastors face heartaches, trials, and difficult obstacles just all other Christians. The difference is, when we go through these trials, our families, church, and friends expect our trials to have no effect on us. In a sense, we hold ourselves accountable for how we react to various situations. Sometimes it is necessary for believers and leaders to stop seeking answers and help from everyone else, look within themselves and their personal relationship with God, and listen to what the Spirit of God is saying to us. We cannot fix every problem. We do not have the power to repair every relationship, or every negative circumstance that take place in our lives. There are times when we even become frustrated over our circumstances. The word of God reminds us in the book of James, chapter 1, verses 2-8 that we should "count it all joy when you fall into various trials" (NKJV), because the trials that we face are strengthening our patience in God. We are also reminded in these verses to practice faith. Whatever we stand in need of, we should ask God to meet those needs and believe that He will do it.

What else do the aforementioned chapters in the book of James tell us? Not only should we *stop* worrying about trials we suffer, but we should have Joy because God is working in our lives, through our trials. If we *look* to God for help us through our trials and believe that He will do it, it will be done. The word of God tells us to "pray without ceasing" (1 Thessalonians 5:17, NKJV). When we pray, we are looking to God for answers. Our walk with Jesus is a daily walk, therefore we must pray daily, sometimes hourly. This verse tells us to continue to *look* to God. Most, if not all, ministers and pastors pray daily. We are to pray about everything. I have not met a minister who does not pray constantly. Before we begin our day, we pray, during the day we pray, and in every in every decision we must make, we go before God in prayer. The question here is, are we taking time out to stop, look, and listen to what the

Spirit of God is saying, or are we praying and still attempting to solve our problems.

We know that God's time is not our time. We cannot decide when something will take place in our lives. We can put forth the work such as planning to build, seeking employment, or implementing a new program in the church, but it will not come to pass, until God says so. We become frustrated when our desires, goals, and projects do not happen in our time. Continue to pray and look to God. Sometimes the things we want or desire most are not the things that God want us to have.

What happens when we stop, trying to handle every situation on our own and look to God for direction and answers? God shows up! Next, we must listen to what the Spirit of God is telling us when He shows up. Do you recognize the voice of the Lord? As leaders, are you certain that you are following the voice of God? How can you obey the voice of God, if you do not know His voice? The answer is simple. You can't.

The Chosen: Answering God's Call on your Life

I can remember when I did my initial sermon. I was not sure what I was supposed to wear. I begin to pray about that. I did not run around shopping trying to find the perfect outfit. I prayed and sought direction from the Lord. The Lord spoke to me. He spoke to my spirit. I could hear Him because I was seeking and patiently waiting on Him. One day, as I was meditating, the voice of the Lord spoke to me and told me to wear all white, and wear a white robe to cover my clothes. It was then, that I went shopping and bought a white suite and a white clergy robe.

The week before I was to speak God confirmed to me what He wanted me to wear. One of the elders of the church, an evangelist came to me. She said I know you are getting ready to conduct your initial sermon. Do you have anything white to wear? It was that moment that I knew that God confirmed what I was supposed to wear. As she and I talked. I informed her that I had a white suite. Then she asked, would I like to borrow one of her white robes. I smiled and told her no, I already had one. Wow! Look at God! You see, when God speaks to us and we *listen* and obey Him, He will confirm what He has told us. Confirmation could come through a person, place, or thing. In that situation, confirmation came to me through a person.

Let me give you another example of obeying the voice of God. After I was severely abused by my last husband, I prayed for God to bring me out of that marriage. This was not a marriage that I was supposed to be in to start with. I was never given the approval from God to marry that man. When we act on our emotions, we may find ourselves suffering in a situation that we did not have to be in. I prayed every day to God to make a way for me to move out of the home. I cried myself to sleep more nights than I can remember. There were even times when I asked God what was taking Him so long to move me out. I knew He saw my pain. I also know He was with me. Even when my ex-husband charged at me with a knife, I knew God was with me. The way I was abused, I should have been dead, but God spared my life. He allowed me to experience the pain, so that it would serve as a lesson that I must not act on emotion and wait on Him.

The Chosen: Answering God's Call on your Life

One particular day, my then husband was doing his usual, drinking alcohol and abusing me because I am a Christian and did not agree with him drinking. I can remember sitting in the dining room. Normally, once he began the abuse I would go to my bedroom and close the door. Even though he would come after me, I would always remove myself from his presence. That particular day, I stayed in the dining room. I looked at him as he laughed in my face. I sat there praying to God silently while my then husband called me dozens of derogatory names; I prayed, listened to the voice of God and did not speak back. I knew God was getting ready to move in that situation. My then husband, in his drunken state, went outside to talk with neighbors who had called the authorities. Eventually he was taken into custody. I asked the Lord to show me what to do. I asked God to show me when, and how to move. I dried my face. As I was drying my face, the Spirit of God spoke to me. The Spirit of God told me to go to a local realtor. I had never been to their office; however, I knew where the realtor's office was from passing it from time to time. When I arrived, still upset, and hurt over the situation I was in, I was not sure what to say to them. I went inside. The lady behind the counter said, "May I help you?" I said, "I am looking for a two-bedroom apartment for my son and me." She said, "Well, we have a long list of them; you will have to go through the list, choose one, go look at it and wait to get approved."

My first thought was, "Lord, why am I here? I was in no condition to look through a long list, let alone go out and look at places to live that day. The lady showed me the list and it looked foreign to me. It was as if I could not make out any of the words, but I could still feel the presence of God with me. I chose to look at a two-bedroom townhome. I could not even pronounce the street; however, I informed the lady behind the counter that was the home I wanted to look at. I asked if she could give me directions. Little did I know this street was only blocks from the church I was attending. I even drove past this street every Sunday morning in the church van as I picked up members. I came to the home. Before I opened the door, I prayed. I asked God to show me. I begged God not to leave me. At this point, I felt as if I were all alone.

I turned the key, opened the door, and walked in. Tears begin to fall down my face. I felt a sense of peace in my presence. I walked upstairs and went into the master bedroom. The Spirit of God spoke to me and said, "This is your new room." I sat down in the floor and cried. After about 10 minutes, I got up and walked into the other bedroom. The Spirit of God said, "This is your son's room." Again, I cried. The Spirit of God spoke to me and said, "You must trust me. Do not look at what you have."

After pulling myself together, praying and seeking direction from the Lord, I took the key back to the realtor. I asked her for an application. She said there was an application fee. I had enough money in my wallet at the time, so I paid the fee. The realtor looked at me and asked if I were ok. I told her yes, God is good and I'm going to be ok. I just need a home for my son and me. I completed the application. I asked her how soon she would get back with me. She said it should only take a few days. I thanked her and begin driving back to the apartment that I shared with my ex-husband. As I was driving back, I can recall thanking and praising God for what He had shown me and for what He was going to do.

The Spirit of God spoke to me again, before I made it back to the apartment. God told me to go in and pack. I said, "Ok, Lord. I will obey you." I went in the apartment. I found my son and told him we need to pack; we are moving. He asked me where. I told him God is moving us to a safe place. I described the home to my son; he immediately started packing. We were both packing as fast as we could. I did not tell him I had to wait to hear from the realtor, I did what God told me to do.

As I continued to pack, my phone rang. It was the realtor. She said you have been approved for the home, and asked when I would like to move in. I said tomorrow. She told me to come back the same day and pay the deposit so no one else will get the home. Let me remind you, all of this happened within a few hours' time. I had a problem – or what I thought was a problem. I did not have the deposit. I told the realtor I would be in within the hour. I had no idea where I was going to get the deposit, but I knew I would have the first month's rent the following day. When I hung up the phone, I screamed so loud. My son came in running in the room and asked what was going on. I told him we were moving tomorrow. I called the bank to check the balance on one of my accounts and there was enough money in there to make the deposit! My son and I went to the realtor and paid our deposit. The next morning, I went back and paid the first month's rent. My son and I began to move our things.

As we moved our belongings, I realized I did not have enough money to rent a truck to move. We continued to move what we could in my SUV. My son called his dad, told him we were moving into our new place, and asked if he could help. His dad showed up and was so happy we were moving. He asked me where the truck was. I told him I could not afford a truck, but we are going to take everything we could in my SUV.

He told me to keep packing and he and my son would be right back.

When they returned, he had a moving truck large enough to move all of my furniture! Several men from the neighborhood who knew about the abuse I suffered on more than one occasion, pitched in and helped load the truck. They loaded up everything that belonged to me. That night, my son and I spent the night in our new place and the peace I had could only from God.

God knows our needs. He is in control over every situation in our lives and He is able to bring us out. Even though I had left my ex-husband several times, by fleeing to abused women's shelters, I would always end up going back home because I was so uncomfortable. There is a difference when we move in a situation without waiting on God and when we wait on God to move us. When I stop trying to handle the situation on my own, looked to God for answers, and listened to His voice He was able to move like I couldn't. When God moved set me free from that situation, I never went back.

In the aforementioned situation, God allowed the peace that I felt when I entered the new home to serve as confirmation that He was doing the work. If you find yourself in a constant struggle over a situation, regardless of how severe it may be, stop, look, and listen. Patiently wait on God to work it out for you and I'm a witness that He will change your situation. Once God change your situation, you will not have to wrestle with it again. It is done.

Chapter 8: Hitting the Books

After moving into my new home, I continued with school as I was led by God to do so. Keeping up with my academics became challenging as I proceeded with the divorce. Through faith in God and by allowing Him to comfort me, I was able to complete my bachelor's degree. As of today, I have competed all of the required courses for my master's degree and in the process of completing my internship. I know God has set the course for my life. He as confirmed to me, through His Spirit that obtaining a doctorate degree is His plan for me. He is making a way for me to continue school. There are times, when I feel as if I cannot go on with school, I become frustrated in myself, however it is during those times, I hear the voice of the Lord reminding me, it is not my will, but His will. When you are operating in God's will, you no longer look at *your* abilities.

Approximately a year after moving into my townhome, I was diagnosed with rheumatoid arthritis. I knew something was going on in my body, but I was not sure what it was. I begin to have difficulty climbing the stairs. Sometimes I would crawl up the stairs, simply because of the pain of trying to walk. I still have days when I have to crawl up the stairs. I would sprain my ankle just by stepping out of the bed. My wrist and arms had begun to swell. I was initially diagnosed by my primary care physician, who referred me to a specialist who confirmed the diagnoses. I was also diagnosed with osteoarthritis, and fibromyalgia. I was placed on several medications to help with the symptoms. Regardless of the pain, I continue with school. Graduate level coursework is more rigorous; however, with God all things are possible!

Shortly after my diagnosis from the rheumatologist, I begin to have extreme pelvic pain. It was found that I had multiple cysts on both of my ovaries and a benign tumor. Due to this medical condition, I had to have major surgery right before attending a week-long, on-campus intensive at school. I had several concerns going into surgery. Recovery was one of them; however, my faith was in God. I had major surgery on January 9th, 2012. After spending only one night in the hospital, I was released to recover at home. I thank God for my mother who stayed with me for several days and for my wonderful friends who came by to prepare meals. During my recovery from surgery, I spent my days studying for my upcoming intensive class. Unfortunately, one of the surgical sites became infected, which slowed down the healing process. Initially, the doctor did not approve of me taking a train for five hours, and spending a week away from home. After hearing how determined I was to attend the class, my doctor released me to go with several restrictions, lifting was one of them.

This was a major problem for me. I had to stay a week on campus, meaning I had to take clothing for a week, along with books, and my laptop. My suitcase was very heavy. Although it had wheels on it, it was still heavy to lift on and off the train. I arrived in Lynchburg, VA shortly after 5 am. I struggled with my luggage, as there was no one there to assist me. I continued to struggle as the train pulled off. Soon, I found myself on the platform alone, struggling to push, pull, and carry my luggage. I had called the local taxicab company prior to my arrival and was told a cab would be waiting for me. I did not see anyone. I stopped and stood on the platform thinking to myself, how in the world was I going to make it to the terminal. A few minutes later, I saw a man walking very fast towards me. Finally, he was close enough to me where I could see the jacket he was wearing was from the taxicab company. He said something told him to come down to lower platform to see if I was there and sure enough, there I stood. I thank God for sending help when we needed it. The driver could have assumed that I did not show up, and drove off; instead, God led him to look for me.

I was relieved when the driver showed up. I had begun to have pain from my surgery and desperately needed to get to my hotel room where I could lie down and relax. I arrived at the hotel and was allowed to check in early. I called several of my classmates to let them know I had arrived safely. As always, I called home to let my family know that I had arrived and was relaxing in my hotel room. The pain was increasing, so I took the pain medications the doctor prescribed for me, sat in my room, and watched the beautiful snow-fall. It snowed for hours. The snow-covered mountains were breathtaking. I relaxed in my room for the entire day as I prepared myself for a week long of lectures and afternoon counseling sessions.

Some of the women in my class would check on me periodically to make sure I was not in too much pain and I was eating. As I look back on that trip, I thank God for providing everything I needed at the time I needed it. There was even a classmate who was staying in a room across from me, who carried my laptop and books for me, so I would not hurt myself lifting. She would check on me every evening after class and would call me every morning to make sure I was awake and had breakfast.

After the second day of classes, I was in so much pain from my surgery I wanted to give up. I called a friend and explained to her that I should not have come to the session. I packed my clothes to leave. I realized that I would have been giving up an entire session after completing and passing the pre-course, and passing all pre- test required for me to attend the session. I prayed, asked God for strength, and decided to stay. The rest of the week seemed to have gone by very fast. I was excited on Friday and was ready to return home.

I shared my story of struggling with my luggage with another classmate. She informed me that she drove to campus and would give me a ride to the store, so I could purchase a larger suitcase. We went shopping and I found a large suitcase able to hold all of my belongings. I arrived in Lynchburg with three pieces of luggage and was returning home with four.

I had to wait about an hour for my train to arrive. Once the train arrived, I rolled my luggage to the platform and was ready to board. The attendant told me I had to lift my own luggage onto the train and place it above my seat. I struggled to pull it up the steps. When I was at my seat, there was no way I could lift it. I stood in the isle for a second trying to figure out how I was going to get my luggage above the seat. There were several passengers in the isle who had become frustrated with me because my luggage was blocking the isle. I heard the loud voice of the staff yell at me to put my luggage up and move out of the way. I tried with all of my might to lift it, but could not do it. I heard them yell again, telling me I would have to get off the train if I could not lift my own luggage. Just as I was about to de-board the train a very nice, man told the other passengers to move out of the way, so he could help me. He struggled with the luggage for a second, and then was able to get it securely in the rack above the seat. I thanked him and took my seat. This trip has taught me valuable lesson. God will send help, but I must learn to pack lighter.

I was in severe pain due to my failed attempts of trying to lift my luggage. I took my pain medication, closed my eyes, and begin to thank God for sending me help. You see when you are obedient to God and press your way as you are walking in your calling, God will always send you the help you need at the precise time that you need it. As I look back over my trip, I thank God for being with me the entire time. He never left me. Our walk with Christ and service to Him will not be without some pain and discomfort, but He will always show up, ease our pain, and provide us with the comfort we need. We serve an awesome God!

After arriving home, I continued hit the books. One thing I have learned in the past eight years that I have been in school is that people who do not go to college, are not always understanding of those who do. For example, I have had friends and family members become angry with me because I chose to study, write papers, and focus on my academics as opposed to spending time with them or doing the things they want me to do. This is not to say that I never spend time with my family. I am family oriented and enjoy my time with my family, but when I am in school; my focus is on just that.

I have had friends who became angry with me, when they call and I have to turn down lunch, dinner, or just hanging out having some old-fashioned girl time. They have even asked me to stop writing papers or stop studying long enough to do something fun. It was as if they thought I was not enjoying what I am doing. I have had family members become angry, saying they are tired of me always studying and not making time for family functions. I do make time for family functions when I have time. You cannot excel at something you put your mind to, if you do not put forth the work to finish it.

I have been writing this book for over a year, and have a passion to write. This book is my testimony. It is my testimony of what God has done, is doing, and where He is taking me. My academic endeavors are a part of me answering God's call on my life. I pray that my family and friends will become more understanding. I know as I transition into the final leg of my academics I will be away from my family and friends for almost two years. My prayer is that I will continue to do God's will, and not the will of those who are around me. Even if those who love me the most do not understand that I must fulfill all the works that God has for me, I still will press on and continue to run this race for Christ.

Hitting the books in adulthood has its advantages as well as its disadvantage. My children are grown, so I have more time to study, however as we age, we lose part of our ability to retain information. It makes it more challenging, because you must find ways to help sharpen our memory. If God calls you to preach, teach, or minister, He will qualify you for the work.

As Christians, we are told in the book of second Timothy, chapter two, and verse fifteen to study to show ourselves approved. That studying is not limited to the studying of God's word. If God gives us gifts that require additional studying, we must follow His Spirit and do what He is requiring of us. God will give some the gift of healing through medicine and surgical procedures. In order to fully practice that gift, you must go to medical school. Whatever your calling and gifts are, study the word of God and study the calling. Study the work that you must do. God may want to send you to another country to minister His word. It would benefit you and those whom you are ministering too if you were to learn and study their culture and language. There are people who want to place limits on the work that God can do through them. Again, whom He calls, He will qualify for the work. You do not have to be ashamed because you may not have the knowledge you think you should have. Pray and hit the books! God will allow you to receive all the knowledge necessary to do what He has called you to do!

Chapter 9: Why are we fighting?

The word of God tells us that there is "one Lord, one faith, one Baptism; one God and Father of all, who *is* above all, and through all, and in you all" (Ephesians, 4:5-6, NKJV) so why are we fighting? Why is there so much competition in the body of Christ? Why are the different denominations of believers fighting one another? I will address these questions in the chapter.

As I stated in the previous chapters, I am a non-denominational Christian who loves the Lord. I believe in the gospel of Jesus Christ. I believe in the word of God. I believe that there is life after death and where we spend eternity is based on our acceptance of Jesus Christ and our behaviors as Christians. I believe that we should have no other God's but the Lord and worship Him in Spirit and in truth.

I accepted the Lord as my personal savior when I was eleven years old. I began to study the bible and prayed for understanding of His word. At the age of sixteen, I went before the Lord again and asked to be baptized. I did not want to be baptized as I did when I was a young child, under the direction of my parent's; I chose to accept God and His Holy Spirit for myself and was baptized again at age sixteen.

I believe in God with all my heart and soul. I love others as He loves us. I have been in the company of people from all walks of life and various denominations; however it never interfered with my relationship with God. There were times when I was a child that my aunt would babysit my siblings and me and would dress us in garb and hijab (Muslim attire). She would take us to the moss with her. I never understood their prayers, nor did I participate. I was there as an observer.

Though I was very young when I would visit the moss with my aunt, I knew my beliefs were different from theirs. I never felt a desire to become involved in the Muslim faith. I found their attire interesting. I always asked my aunt questions such as why do the women cover their bodies completely and their heads and faces. I also felt as if the women worshipped their husbands more than God. I saw women bowing before their husbands. Women who were single did not look men in their eyes. There was even a time, out of curiosity, that I found myself looking at what some of the men were doing and my aunt quickly grabbed and turned my face and told me not to look at them. Again, this was my experience when I visited a Sunni mosque. This is not to say that all Muslims practice the same religious principles.

My experience as an adult as I visited various churches and was in the company of others was just as shocking! It seems as if everyone is attempting to out preach or out church (if I may use this analogy) one another. There is an extreme amount of jealousy and competition in the churches. As I visited a non-denominational church where the members were primary Caucasian, the pastor looked at me, smiled, and said we have church like the black people. What! First, that was a racist comment. Our walk with Christ is not about black or white, it's about Jesus. Second, that pastor assumed I had attended predominately African American churches. Third, why was his focus on pleasing man and not God? I was offended by the pastor's remarks, but the spirit of God would not allow me to say anything. Instead, I prayed for him.

Another experience I had with a Baptist church happened when I was invited to pray for members who wanted prayer. As I prayed for a young lady, I could feel the spirit of God begin to move through prayer. The young lady had begun to cry as God was working in her. The prayer was quickly interrupted by another minister! The other minister stopped me from praying with the young lady, and asked that the young lady go to the pastor of the church and get prayer. I never thought I would experience anything like that. I was in shock. The young lady was just as confused as I was. She walked up to the pastor and the pastor asked her if she wanted her to pray for her. The young lady said, "No, I want Evangelist Ree to pray with me."

The problem in these types of situations is simple... jealousy. Some pastors and ministers believe they must be the only ones allowed to pray for others. They do not accept that God can choose whom He want to pray for His children. I could not ignore that situation. I felt uneasy in my spirit. I went to that pastor in private later that day and asked why she had one of her associate ministers interrupt the prayer. She stated that she wanted to ask the young lady who she wants to pray for her. I told her, the young lady asked me to pray for her, I felt the spirit of God leading me to pray for her, so I did. At that point, the pastor stated, if I want to become pastor of her church, she will gladly step down. My thought was WHERE IN THE WORLD DID THAT COME FROM? Lord knows I did not desire to become a pastor.

There were numerous occasions that I have been asked to do certain works in a church and the pastors have tried to make me feel as if I am less than what God has called me to be. Some pastors and church leaders will try to control the Spirit of God in you. They do not want you to do God's will they would rather you follow their plans, rules, and objectives. The spirit of God in me will not allow others to affect my walk and service to Christ. I have talked to countless ministers, evangelist, and teachers of the Gospel who have experienced similar if not worse situations. If God has called you to do His work and you know that your calling is of God, you cannot allow man/woman to deter you from doing what thus says the Lord. Too many people are walking away from the church and God because they have experienced such abuse and rejection from pastors and church leaders.

I can understand pastors and leaders wanting to protect the house of God. Senior pastors have the right to say who can and who cannot speak in the house of God in which they have been appointed over. In some cases, pastors will not allow you to speak in their appointed churches unless you attend a certain amount of classes set up by them. In other cases, you may be required to have a degree in theology or divinity before you are even considered worthy or qualified to speak, let alone lead a congregation. The word of God tells us that the Holy Spirit is our teacher (John, 14:26 and Luke 12:12, NKJV). We can learn from textbooks, but the word of God and His Spirit, must be our ultimate teacher. We must live according to the word of God and we must preach the gospel according to the calling that is on our lives, not according to man's rules and restrictions.

These are ways that so many ministers have been hurt by churches. Some ministers will search different churches until they find one where the pastor/leader is so comfortable with His calling, he will allow God's children to practice their gifts under his leadership. A pastor who is confident in his/her relationship with God and the anointing that is on their lives are not intimated by the anointing on someone else's life. We can all learn from one another. You may have a mega church with thousands of members, but you can still learn something and be blessed through any anointed minister of God. The size of the church God has placed you in does not give you the power to abuse His children nor control their gifts. After all, God is in control of all!

If we examine the churches twenty-five to fifty years ago, you would not see the kinds of divisions you see today. The modern churches have walked away from their true purpose. God's houses across the world are set up for God's children to go and be healed. I can recall when I was a young girl between the ages of six through eleven. I would go into the church and preachers were preaching about deliverance, salvations, and the power of God. Souls were being saved. People were getting free of the worldly bondages they were in. Yes, my mother dressed my sisters and me in cute little pink dresses with frilly socks, and pink ribbons in our hair. My brothers wore suits and ties. Sunday was a time for the family to come together, worship the Lord, and afterward, spend time with one another.

My mother dressed us that way, to instill in us a sense of respect for God's house. We were taught to respect the house of God in every way. We did not chew gum, text on cell phones, or play in the seats. We listened to the men of God as they preached the Gospel. At the age of six, I knew Jesus died for me. I could feel the anointing and the presence of God even at six years old. I watched ministers fall out in the floor giving in to the power of God. I was not afraid, as some children may have been. I can remember one Sunday tears rolled down my face as I listened to one of the pastors preach about the power of God and the love of Jesus. I cried because I felt that anointing in me. I was afraid if I got up, my mother would quickly sit me back down; after all, I was only six years old, so I sat there. I can recall leaving church with my family and going home and still feeling the presence of God with me. I would go into closets and hiding places throughout the house and begin to pray. At that time, I was not sure what to pray for, so I begin to tell God, "I believe."

I welcomed the spirit of God in my life at an early age. I went to church every chance I had. Even during the times when my family stop going to church, I would always find someone to go to church with. My siblings and friends teased me because I was so different. Sometimes I did not understand why I was so different. Now, I know. I was not only called by God, I was chosen. Do not fight against me because God has called me to do His work. We must accept that God calls more than just us. There is no need for Christians to fight amongst each other. There is enough God for all of us

Do not fight against those who labor among you. You never know how God is going to use them in your life or in your ministry. Answering the call on our lives is accepting and submitting to the power of God. As Christians, we are to work together to help those who are lost, hurting and in need; we must possesses the spiritual knowledge to discern who we allow minister to us. The word of God reminds us in the book of 1st John chapter verse four, verses one through five to "try the spirits" (NKJV). We must make sure that those who are ministering to us are of God. If our spirits agree, there should not be fighting. We should be working together so one day we all can hear Him say, well done.

While writing this chapter, I conducted a small survey from one of today's most popular websites today; Facebook. In conducting the survey, I wanted to get a better understanding of why there is so much division among believers. I surveyed members from various denominations. Some are Baptist, others are non-denominational, Muslim, Apostolic, Methodist, Pentecostal Holiness, and from the co-exist movement. I presented the participants with the same five questions. Question one asked the participants, about their denomination. Question two asked the age of the participant. Question three asked about the participant's religion or spiritual beliefs. Question four asked at what age they first began to practice their beliefs. Question five asked the participants about their feelings towards members of other denominations.

I surveyed both women and men ranging in ages from nineteen years old to fifty-seven years old, with an average age of thirty-seven years old. The answers to both questions one and two varied as the participants were from different denominations and different ages. There were some similarities and some differences with question three. Ninety percent of the participants believed in God, the Trinity, and the gospel of Jesus Christ. Those of the Muslim faith professed that they believe in God, but not Jesus. And one participant believe that people get out of life what they put into it. On question four, ninety-nine percent of the participants reported they began practicing their beliefs as a child or in young adulthood by parents or other family members.

Evangelist Ree Holmes-Monserrate

On question five, all of the participants answered; they are accepting of others from different denominations, as long as they are positive beliefs and are not harming others. My question again, after conducting the survey is why are we fighting?

Here is why so many are fighting; everyone believes their faith and biblical teachings are the ultimate truths. Our walk and service to Christ is personal. Everyone must have a personal relationship with God for themselves. Once we develop a personal relationship with our Lord and savior, then we have the responsibility to help others come to know Christ. Here is where you will see various disagreements; denominations are sets of man-made traditions and practices. Some may worship in one way; others may worship in another. Some denominations of believers have various interpretations of the word of God. I have been in churches that do not believe in women in the ministry. They will read scriptures, such as that of 1st Timothy chapter two, verses 11-15, (NKJV) where the apostle Paul delivered a message to his brother Timothy concerning women remaining silent in the church and not speaking. Many will use this particular scripture to say that God does not call women to preach and Jesus does not use women in the ministry. This is not so.

Paul was teaching Timothy how to restore order and peace in the church of Ephesus. There were those who were teaching false doctrine and behaving in ways that were not pleasing to God. Paul, a minister of the God went to Timothy, as any of us would do if we knew a fellow brother or sister in Christ was allowing disorder in the church and spoke to him concerning the things that were taking place in the churches of Ephesus. There were women who were teaching false doctrine as well as men who were not living a life pleasing to God. Paul was instructing Timothy as to how to regain peace in the church. Let's take a look at what Paul said to Timothy. "And I do not permit a woman to teach or to have authority over a man, but to be in silence" (1st Timothy 2:12, NKJV). This was Paul's advice to Timothy. In other words, if they do not know the truth, it is better for them to keep quiet.

Evangelist Ree Holmes-Monserrate

When we study the word of God, we must study the author of the book, the audience to whom the author is addressing and the messages or teachings of the author. The bible is written by God's chosen. We must remember that not every message written in the bible applies to the modern church. We are no longer living under the Law of Moses, but under the dispensation of grace and through Jesus Christ and His teachings.

Let's take another very controversial subject that has been receiving a great deal of attention both in and out of church, the subject of homosexuality. Why are Christians fighting over the choice that someone has made to live a homosexual life? Yes, I said *choice*. Many people have experienced homosexual relationships. Some who feel as if they were born with a gene that makes them more attracted to the same sex? Well… it is possible to be born with a gene that makes you more attracted to the same sex, but what does the word of God say concerning relationships with someone of the same sex?

The Chosen: Answering God's Call on your Life

Homosexuality was first addressed in the book of Leviticus, under the law of Moses, which states that men should not lie with other men as they would with a female (Leviticus, 18:22, NKJV). Now let's look at what the new testament of Jesus says concerning this subject, 1st Corinthians 6: 9-10, which is also believed to be written by the Apostle Paul. In this chapter and verse, Paul is speaking to the church, of Corinth in which he founded. In this particular scripture, Paul speaks about a number of abominations against God that would prohibit one from entering into the Kingdom of God. Homosexuality is one of those abominations.

Paul also delivered a powerful message to those who commit such abominations. In the book of Romans, also believed to have been written by the Apostle Paul, chapter one, verses twenty-six through twenty eight, Paul ministers to the word to the church saying that those who practice such abominations, are going to do so regardless of the word of God, so God gave them the desires of their hearts. Their *choice* to submit to their own desires, was greater than the decision to serve the Lord with their minds, bodies, and souls, therefore, "God gave them over to a depraved mind" (verse 28, NKJV). There is no reason for Christians to argue with those whom God has allowed to practice in err, and will ultimately judge them.

Today, we see so many people arguing over what is right and what is wrong. Stop arguing! Develop a personal relationship with God for yourself and allow the Lord to direct your steps. We are all sinners saved by grace. Instead of arguing, we should be living our lives according to Jesus Christ' greatest commandments which are to love the Lord your God with all your heart, with all your soul and all of your mind and the second is to love your neighbor as you love yourself (Matt 22:36, NKJV).

Churches our time is limited, do not argue, love. Believers, our time is limited, do not argue, love. Pastors, ministers, and leaders around the world, our time is limited, do not argue, love. The love of Jesus Christ should be shown in everything we do. If others do not show the love of Christ, their sins are not yours to bear.

You do not have to accept any other religious beliefs, denominations, practices, or lifestyles, just love as we all have been commanded to do. You can love without accepting other's beliefs, but you cannot believe in God and Jesus Christ without loving all of His children. I love you all.

Chapter 10: The Chosen

What does it mean to be chosen by God? Who are God's chosen? Let's go back to the opening scripture of this book Matthew 22:14 "for many are called, but few are chosen. Just as a parent call on their children to follow the rules of their house, God has called His children to abide by His rules. When you accept Jesus Christ as your personal Lord and savior, you are saying yes God, I believe you are the creator of all things, I believe you created the heavens and the earth. I believe you sent your only son, in the form of man, which is Jesus to suffer the cross and die for my sins, and I believe that you send your Holy Spirit to guide me to righteousness.

When we look at called from that aspect, we can see that the scripture is accurate many are called! Millions, even billions are called to serve the Lord. What about those who are chosen? When you look at the process of being chosen, you are being selected to do a certain task. In the ministry, God chose Abraham to do His work, God chose Moses to lead His people, and God chose those who would deny themselves to do His work. Just as God chose certain believers to perform certain works, Jesus, who is of God also choose certain believers to do the task of His work for the perfecting of the saints. How did Jesus choose? He chose by bestowing certain gifts on both men and women of God. Ephesians 4:11: "and He gave some Apostles, and some prophets, and some evangelists, and some pastors and teachers" (KJV) describes the gifts in which were placed on those whom He has called and those whom He chose.

The aforementioned gifts are not to say that only those who are in the ministry are chosen. Many believers possess gifts from God, who deny themselves and serve Him with their whole heart, using their gifts for the glory of God. Just as many are called to do the work of God, there are also many false teachers and false prophets. We know this because of the word of God warns us to be aware of them in the book of Matthew, chapter seven, verses fifteen through twenty. The word of God describes them as "wolves in Sheep's clothing" (KJV).

Evangelist Ree Holmes-Monserrate

When you think of a wolf, you think of a powerful and dangerous animal. God sends us a powerful message that there are people in the world today who possess this type of dangerous power. They will appear to be of God, but will lack the power that God gives His chosen. The power that God gives is the power of the Holy Spirit. This power includes the power to lay hands on the sick so they may be healed, the power to correct our thoughts and behaviors, and the power to discern right from wrong. Why did I say they have dangerous power? There are pastors, ministers, evangelist, Apostles, and teachers appointed by men over churches and congregations who are not chosen by God. They are crafty. They know how to turn the word of God into a tool of manipulation for their personal gain. They may preach a sermon, they may pray over the sick; they may even become financially wealthy, but their work is for their benefit, not for the kingdom of God and His people. So, how do we know they are not of God? The word of God tells us that we will know them by their fruits Matthew 7:16 (NKJV).

The Chosen: Answering God's Call on your Life

Good trees from the Lord, brings forth good
fruit (Matt 7:17, NKJV). A chosen man or woman of
God will above all things, love God and keep His commandments. They will preach love; they will practice
love, and show love. The works from their hands will
be good work. God's chosen do not live their lives to
please man. We live to please God. God's chosen know
that we must at times, give up the things we enjoy for
the good of our brother or sister or for the betterment
of life. When you are chosen by God, you will fast for
the healing of other. You will give up eating food so
that you can be filled with the Holy Ghost and be in a
position for God to use you.

Many times, when we think about getting in
position for God to use us, we think about physical
places as well as spiritual places, but we do not always
think about the supernatural position that God desires
us to be in. When Jesus disciples asked Him, how He
was able to heal certain diseases and raise the dead, Jesus answered them and said this kind of healing can
only come through fasting and praying (Mark 9:22,
NKJV). This is to say, there are some among us who will

need us to be empty of every substance except the Holy Spirit, so they may be delivered. This is part of the task we must do as God's chosen.

As God's chosen, we cannot choose which task we will do and what task we will not do. We must do as thus says the Lord. Many have been called, but few are chosen (Matt 22:14, NKJV). Many will preach the Gospel, do good works, feed their brother or sister, love their neighbor, but how many will turn over their plate for a friend? Now days, we take some much medication that we fear that fasting from food will cause us to become sick. Where is your faith? The medications I take for my various ailments require that I take them with food, but when I go into fasting and praying, I allow the Lord to guide me. The Spirit of God orders my steps. When obeying the Spirit, I know when to fast, how to fast, and how long to fast. It is not up to man as to how long I fast and the things that I am to fast from. There are times, when the Lord will have me fast from food and only drink water. Just as my relationship with God is personal, so is my practice of fasting and praying so the Lord can use me.

The Chosen: Answering God's Call on your Life

When we as the chosen allow God to work through us, the fruit we will see is healing, deliverance, and broken bonds. As aforementioned there are more pastors and leaders fasting and praying for financial prosperity than that of healing and deliverance, but as we are taught, what does it profit anyone to gain the world and lose his soul (Matt 16:26, NKJV). No money in the world can buy salvation. Financial prosperity cannot buy peace. It was once said that the best things in life are free. This is true. Salvation is free, all we have to do is believe, accept Jesus, and be baptized according to the word of God. Peace comes with accepting the Lord through any situation you may face.

While writing this book, I had a situation arise that made me very uncomfortable. I was told that there was an abnormality on my mammogram. My immediate thought was breast cancer, as my mother experienced breast cancer twice. I believed I was at a higher risk. I begin to think on other family members who suffered from various forms of cancer and these thoughts brought about sadness in my heart. I begin to cry as I thought about the things in which my family suffered

110

and what I thought was going on in my body. I stretched out on my bed in tears, I called several friends so that we could touch and agree in prayer for healing. I was not comforted by anything my friends were saying to me. As I continued to cry, I found myself on the floor beside my bed. I pulled my body up so that I was on my knees. It was in that position that the Lord stepped in and whispered softly to me, that's enough! When the Spirit of God speaks to you, His words are clear, but bold.

I begin to pray for healing, and the Spirit of God spoke to me and said you are not sick. You do not have cancer. I begin to pray for strength. A dear friend and Apostle reminded me that the joy of the Lord is my strength. You see, God will place people in your life to help you on your walk and service to Christ. I already knew the joy of the Lord is my strength, but sometimes, negative circumstances that come up in our lives, can temporarily block our thinking. Then I begin to pray for joy. I prayed to God that He would allow His joy to strengthen me while I faced whatever it was I had to face. The more I prayed for joy, the more strength the Lord gave me.

On the day I was to return to the doctor for more testing, I was nervous, but I made up in my mind that I wanted Jesus alone to be with me. I had friends who volunteered to go with me, but there are times in our lives that we need to let God be God. He is all the comfort we need. As I sat in the waiting room I noticed all the women were accompanied by their husbands, significant others, and family members. I sat by myself, but I was not alone. God was with me.

Approximately fifteen minutes had passed by and women were beginning to come out of the treatment area. I remember one woman came out in tears. She sat in the seat across from me and was comforted by the arms of her husband. I looked down at my hands and they were shaking. I begin to pray. I asked God to comfort me. I invited the Holy Spirit to sit with me. I closed my eyes as I welcomed the Holy Spirit. I could feel the presence of God. I begin to thank God for answering my prayers. Even during that time, I heard the voice of the enemy as well. When you are of God, you can recognize the voice of God as well as the voice of the enemy. The voice of the enemy said you are alone; you do not have anybody here with you. You are having a panic attack. I immediately begin to plead and apply the blood Jesus over my life and what was to take place in the exam room. You see, the enemy will use your circumstance to his advantage if you allow him. I did not give him that chance. The enemy only has power if we give it to him.

After pleading and applying the blood of Jesus over my life, the shaking in my hands stopped, my heart beat begin to slow down to a normal pace, and I felt peace in my spirit. The technician called my name and ushered me to the exam area. As I waited in small room, I begin to thank God for being with me. I begin to thank God for being everything I need and will need. I begin to sing songs of praise. About twenty minutes later, the technician came to get and begin the test. She explained the procedures and what she was going to do. While she was performing the painful procedure, tears rolled down my face. She asked me was I ok? I said yes, God is good all the time. Even during our pain, He is still good. After the procedure, I was taken back to the waiting area. The technician came back in and I was told they had to do more test. I was then moved to another testing area. Another painful procedure, more tears, more God.

Finally, the doctor came in the room and explained that I have a cyst and it was not cancer. I was told I had to be rechecked in six months. I smiled because I know it was God who is in control over my life. You see that experience reminded me that God is everything I need and He will never leave me. The same God that brought me through major surgery a year prior to this situation brought me through this. He is faithful and will bring me through whatever I may face in the future. It is with praise in my heart and spirit that I can write to you, that at the end of the six months waiting period, I was re-checked and what the spot or cyst they previously saw, is gone!! Giving God all the praise.

Evangelist Ree Holmes-Monserrate

With every situation I face, I always ask God, what would you like me to say? How do you want me to use this as a testimony of your love, grace, and mercy? God showed me that there would be many women who will have to face difficult situations and will only have Him to lean on. I must be a witness and tell them, God is all they need and they can overcome. Some women ministers and even pastors would not want to face the situations that I had to face and go through them without a husband, or family member. I was chosen. I had to go through this without family and friends, because my experience will help one of my sister's or brother's in the future. When we are living for God we are never alone. We may be physically shaken by the things we may face, but they will not break us and through Christ, we will overcome them.

The joy, peace, and comfort I received from God, cannot be bought with money. You cannot put a price tag on faith. Your faith is made strong by trusting in the word and Spirit of God. We must trust and believe that God is with us at all times. There may be times when you do not feel God in your life, but if you are saved and living according to the word, He is always there.

Those who are chosen to do God's work will be placed in uncomfortable situations and may go through pain, but your pain is not in vain. God is positioning you to do His work. Our tasks are not always easy. We all would love to feed those who are hungry, help provide clothes to those who are poor, and preach the word of God, but there are times, at any point in our service to God that He will place us in certain situations, it could be our health, the health of our loved ones, our homes and other situations when we must depend solely on the Lord to bring us out. He will always bring us out. Not only that, He will give us a new song, fresh anointing, and new mercies. I have been ministering the Gospel of Jesus for over sixteen years and I thank God that no matter what I face, He will always bring me out! You are not only called to endure this race, you are chosen!! Do not give up. Do not question God as to why you are going through. Ask God how you can use the situation you are in to glorify Him. Stay humble to the Lord. Do not be overtaken by the things of this world, your health, your circumstances, or any other influences, remember (Phil 2:13, NKJV) it is God who works in you. You are chosen; now let Him work! To God be the glory!

Conclusion

When I began this journey to write to you, I was not sure of the contents the Lord was going to bring out. There were days I wanted to write, but the words were not there. It was during those times that the Lord wanted me to listen before I wrote. God chose specific contents for me to write to you. Even during the final chapter of the book, it could not be written until God positioned me to write it. I had to experience those things so that my testimony could be told. This book is not about my life. This book is about the love of God and how He uses those whom He called and chose to do His work.

From the time the Lord called and chose me to do His work, I have sought direction and order from Him. There were various men and women, who have tried to keep me from the calling that is on my life, but they did not give it to me and they cannot take it away. There are also those who encourage me to continue my service to God regardless of what I may face. I thank God for the pastor's and Apostle's, women and men of

Evangelist Ree Holmes-Monserrate

Him whom He has used to help and assist me on my walk and service to Christ.

As you have read, from the beginning of the book, it was not I who called me, but the Lord who chose me. God did not only call me to be an evangelist of His word, He placed in me ministries that will come forth in His time, most recently the ministry of Woman 2 Woman. W2W Ministries began in September 2012 with a vision to reach women around the world. The group is a support group for Christian women around the globe. There are no specific churches or denominations associated with W2W, we are women who love the Lord and are willing to allow the Lord to use us to help our sisters. The vision, including the name was given to me by the Lord. The meetings have blessed many women and God is given the glory. While sharing my vision with my dear friend Mrs. Cristol Houey, she said to me that she was given a similar if not identical vision. Together, with God leading us, we began W2W ministries.

The Chosen: Answering God's Call on your Life

Recently the Lord spoke to me concerning Woman 2 Woman Ministries. His voice again with authority said to me that I am holding you responsible for the women that attend Woman 2 Woman. I asked God, what does that mean. He said you must teach the truth at all times. If they are not taught the truth, you will be held responsible. Although I have yet to be named pastor of Woman 2 Woman, I live up to the responsibilities that the Lord has placed on me. I have a responsibility to live and teach the truth. If those who attend do not accept the truth, that is their responsibility. I do not have the power to save them, but have been given the authority by God to teach them.

I have also seen the vision of how God is going to use me in the mental health field. Many mental health issues can be resolved by allowing God to come in and rejecting those things, thoughts, and images that are not of God. Again, God is positioning me to do those works. I thank and praise God for how He is using me in the lives of my sisters and brothers in Christ and how He will continue to use me in the future.

Evangelist Ree Holmes-Monserrate

The chosen is not the first book I have written, however it is the first that God had me to write for publication. You see, sometimes God will allow you the experience before placing you in certain positions. I do not desire to be more than what God has called and chosen me to be and I do not desire to be less. I love the Lord with my whole heart and pray that as you have read this book, you would have examined areas in your life and understand that when you are called and chosen to do the work of the Lord, your journey will not always be easy. It may even be hard and painful at times, but your faith and your personal relationship with God will always bring you through.

The chosen was not written to attack anyone. It is written so that pastor's, ministers, leaders, and Christians around the world will examine themselves and make sure they are carrying out the will of God and not become subject to doing their own will. My personal experiences with various churches may not have been all positive, but they were necessary. God allowed me to experience the negative things that are taken places in churches today, so that, one, I can pray for them and two, I will not submit to those types of practices. He has also allowed me to witness the true loving word of God through powerful men and women who are keeping the faith.

Our walk and service to Christ is not about how much we can tear one another down, it is about how much we as a family can encourage one other. Ministry is not all glitz and glamour. There is blood, sweat, and tears, but God is always present. Let us continue to walk with God and love unconditionally those who labor among us as well as those who come to us to learn of the truth. Let us not take credit for the work God is doing in our lives, but humble ourselves and give Him the credit that is due to Him. Do not waiver in your faith. Stay strong. You can endure your trials through the blood of Jesus. After all, you are not only called. You are chosen! To God be the glory!

Evangelist Ree Holmes-Monserrate

About the Author

Evangelist Ree Holmes-Monserrate was born in Washington, DC in 1969. She is the mother of three children Jessica, Darnell, and James, and the grandmother of four. She earned her Bachelor's degree in psychology from Converse College in Spartanburg, SC, and is scheduled to graduate from Liberty University with a Master's degree in professional counseling in December of 2014. Afterward, she will continue her post graduate work on her PsyD and plan to open a Christian based counseling and therapy center. She is a member of the American Association of Christian Counselors. She is also the author of the unpublished works "Just as I am" (Ree's memoir) and "It's Personal: Your Personal Relationship with God." In her spare time, she enjoys playing tennis and relaxing on the beach.

In 2012, Evangelist Ree Holmes-Monserrate gave birth to Woman 2 Woman Ministries a ministry that spreads the love of Jesus Christ around the world through sisterhood. W2WM serves as a mentor to young girls in their walk with Christ as well as support to woman of all ages through life's difficult challenges. Evangelist Ree Holmes-Monserrate loves to serve the people of God and gives God all the glory. For He, alone, is worthy.

Made in the USA
Columbia, SC
24 May 2023

16759290R00070